Justin H. (Justin Huntly) McCarthy

Hafiz in London

Justin H. (Justin Huntly) McCarthy

Hafiz in London

ISBN/EAN: 9783337188429

Printed in Europe, USA, Canada, Australia, Japan

Cover: Foto ©ninafisch / pixelio.de

More available books at **www.hansebooks.com**

HAFIZ IN LONDON

HAFIZ IN LONDON

BY

JUSTIN HUNTLY McCARTHY, M.P.

اکر بزلف دراز تو دست ما نرسد
کناه بخت پریشان و دست کوته ماست

London
CHATTO & WINDUS, PICCADILLY
1886

DEDICATION.

FERANGIS, at thy feet I lay
    These roses from the haunted coast
    Of Faristan, whose poets boast
Their Rocknabad and Mosellay ;
For I was in Shiraz to-day,
    With ancient Hafiz for my host,
    Who, like a comfortable ghost,
With Persian roses crowned my stay.
They are thy tribute from the land
    Of Khayyam and our Khalifate,
    For on their crimson folds of fate
A wizard ciphered with his wand
    Words which I dare not here translate,
But you will read and understand.

CONTENTS.

	PAGE
HAFIZ IN LONDON .	1
MEMORY .	6
ELD	11
LONG AGO . .	14
VANITY . . .	19
KAIF .	21
YOU AND I	25
CONSOLATION	28
LOTUS	31
PHILOSOPHY FOR OTHERS .	33
WISDOM	36

Contents

	PAGE
Renunciation	38
After Rhamazan	40
Lonely	44
Courage	47
Vine-Visions	49
A Dream	52
Attar of Love	58
Vaulting Ambition	60
A Night-Piece	62
Fallen Angels	65
Praise of Wine	67
Haroun er-Rasheed's Poet	70
Ghazel	74
The Grave of Omar-i-Khayyam	77
Omar Answers	86

HAFIZ IN LONDON.

HAFIZ IN LONDON.

Hafiz in London! even so.
For not alone by Rukni's flow
The ruddy Persian roses grow.

Not only 'neath the cypress groves,
With soul on fire the singer roves,
And tells the laughing stars his loves.

Hafiz in London

Here in this city—where I brood
Beside the river's darkling flood,
And feed the fever in my blood

With Eastern fancies quaintly traced
On yellow parchment, half effaced
In verses subtly interlaced—

Men eat and drink, men love and die,
Beneath this leaden London sky,
As eastward where the hoopoos fly,

And through the tranquil evening air
A muezzin from the turret stair
Summons all faithful souls to prayer.

HAFIZ IN LONDON

And we who drink the Saki's wine
Believe its juice no less divine
Than filled, Hafiz, that cup of thine.

Master and most benign of shades,
Before thy gracious phantom fades
To Mosellay's enchanted glades,

Breathe on my lips, and o'er my brain
Some comfort for thy child, whose pain
Strives as you strove, but strives in vain.

When sundown sets the world on fire,
The music of the Master's lyre
Deadens the ache of keen desire.

Hafiz in London

Reading this painted Persian page,
Where, half a lover, half a sage,
You built your heart a golden cage,

My fancy, skimming southern seas,
Wanders at twilight where the breeze
Flutters the dark pomegranate trees.

We all are sultans in our dreams
Of gardens where the sunlight gleams
On fairer flowers and clearer streams;

And thus in dreams I seek my home
Where dim Shiraz, dome after dome,
Smiles on the water's silver foam;

The dancing girls, with tinkling feet
And many-coloured garments, beat
Their drums adown the twisted street;

And while the revel sways along,
The scented, flower-crowned, laughing throng
Seem part and parcel of thy song.

Hafiz, night's rebel angels sweep
Across the sun ; I pledge you deep,
And smiling, sighing, sink to sleep.

MEMORY

SITTING silent in the twilight, faces of my former loves
Float about my fancy softly, like a silver flight of doves.

Brighter than the stars of heaven is the shining of their eyes,
Sweeter are their angel voices than the speech of Paradise.

MEMORY

I am old and grey and weary, winter in my blood and brain;
But to-night these haunting phantoms conjure up my youth again.

Lovingly I name them over, all that world of gracious girls,
Almond-eyed and jasmine-bosomed, like a poet stringing pearls.

In my tranquil cypress mazes just outside the sleepy town,
Blooms a tribe of laughing lilies fairer than a kingly crown.

Every lily in the garden wears a woman's gracious
 name,
Every lily in the garden set my spirit once aflame;

And amongst that throng of lilies scarcely whiter than
his hair,
Hafiz sits and dreams at sunset of the flowers no longer
fair;

Of the sweethearts dead and buried whom I worshipped
long ago,
When this beard as grey as ashes was as sable as the
sloe.

Memory

I would weep if I were wiser, but the idle child of song
Leaves reflection to the Mullah, sorrow to the Sufi throng.

Am I wrong to be contented in the sunlight to rehearse
Pleasant tales of love and lovers in my honey-laden verse?

While the vinepress with the life-blood of the purple clusters drips,
I forget how slowly, surely, day by day to darkness slips,

Heedless how beyond the gateway in the field the nations jar,
Hand on throat and hand on sabre in the trampled lanes of war.

Ah! 'tis better on this pleasant river bank to lie reclined,
While the ghosts of old affections fill the harem of my mind.

Think no more of love and lasses, Hafiz; you can scarcely hold
The Koran with trembling fingers. Hafiz, you are growing old.

ELD.

Hafiz, you are growing old;
    Hafiz, all the girls abandon
Bards whose blood is getting cold,
    Bards whom Time has laid his hand on.
All the merry songs you sung
In the days when you were young,
Are not worth a feather's weight
To arrest the fist of Fate
    When it jogs your shifting sand on.

Hafiz, though a tinge of grey
    Shames the locks that once were sable,
Drink and laugh the world away,
    Swear that eld's a housewife's fable;
Vow that youth is always yours
While the graceful gait allures,
While the perfume haunts the rose,
While a ruddy balsam flows
    From the flagon on the table.

Just a word within your ear,
    Hafiz: you're a craven creature
If you waste a single tear
    On the thought that every feature

Of the fairest face a maid
Ever showed the sun must fade ;
Rather bid your mistress weigh
Youth and beauty's barren stay,
   And a wiser lesson teach her.

Tell her youth was made for love ;
   Tell her wine was made for drinking ;
Tell her that in heaven above
   Mahmoud and his saints are winking
At the golden jest of youth ;
Tell her wisdom's wisest truth
Is, be merry while you may,
Cease regretting yesterday,
   Or about to-morrow thinking.

LONG AGO.

ALL my youth's desires are buried,
 Each within its narrow grave;
Long ago their ghosts were ferried
 O'er Jaihun's enchanted wave;
 Wild ambitions bright and brave,
 Loves that made me serve a slave,
All have slipped away like snow
  Long ago.

Stars in which my youth delighted
   Vanish from the heavenly band,
And I wander a benighted
   Stranger in a stranger land ;
   There is no one left to stand
   By my side or take my hand,
Of the friends I worshipped so
      Long ago.

One sweet name of all the number
   Haunts the chambers of my brain,
One sweet shape disturbs my slumber,
   Loved too well and loved in vain.
   Ah, Ferangis! give again
   Half the pleasure, all the pain,

That my boyhood used to know
    Long ago.

These are dreams: I must remember
    That my youthful days are dead,
That the rigours of December
    Grizzle e'en a poet's head.
    Gone is gone, and dead is dead,
    And no roses bloom as red
As the roses used to blow
    Long ago.

Though my eyes pursue the swallow
    As he travels towards the sun,

Aged limbs refuse to follow
   Where the fancies lightly run.
   Hafiz, cease, the game is done,
   Life's fantastic robe is spun ;
Fate marked out the way to go
      Long ago.

You were passionate, my poet,
   In your manhood's golden dawn ;
Seized the seed of life to sow it
   On the tulip-tinted lawn ;
   Now you sit at home and yawn,
   Withered, grizzled, bent and drawn,
By the hearth : you scorned its glow
      Long ago.

What is left? a sigh, a shudder,
    For my past, and for the goal
Where, a boat without a rudder,
    Drifts my tempest-troubled soul;
    Ah! death's angel, taking toll,
    Shall I find within thy bowl
Better wine than used to flow
    Long ago?

VANITY.

I DREAMT all night of your cold caresses;
   Your kisses froze on my lips like flakes
   Of pitiless snow that chills and breaks
The warm heart snared in your sombre tresses.

I woke with a groan in the livid morning,
   Groaned and swore I would break away
   From the bitter bondage of love, and repay
Laughter with laughter, and scorn with scorning.

Ere noon was hot in the heavens, I met you ;
   You had but to smile as you passed, and lo !
   I was your lover again.   Heigho !
Hate you or love you, I can't forget you.

KAIF.

MINE be the musk and the music, mine be the laughing
	girl ;
　Mine be the ample flagon, brimmed with the blood
	　of the vine ;
Mine the divan encushioned, watching the dancers twirl ;
　Mine the narghili serpent, breathing its soul divine.

Others can juggle with statecraft, others can lust for
	command ;
　Others can envy their fellows woman or vintage or
	　gold ;

Others can wrangle for title, fight for a rood of land ;
  Others think souls and bodies things to be bought and sold.

Such as they are, God made them ; such as they are, God guides ;
  Such as they are, they do their task, fill place in the world awhile ;
Such as they are, they eat and drink, and sleep on the breasts of their brides ;
  Such as they are, they sicken and die—may jackals their graves defile.

I for my part am happy, I for my part am calm,
  I for my part rejoice to the full in the hour that glideth by,

I for my part with all my heart delight in the vineyard's balm,
   I for my part will love and laugh till my moment comes to die.

Grant me, Allah, digestion ; grant me, Allah, desire ;
   Grant me a mistress with almond eyes and cinnamon-scented breath ;
Grant me a golden vessel filled with the vineyard's fire ;
   Grant me, Allah, a lazy life, and later a lazy death.

Dearest, I once was foolish ; dearest, I once was young ;
   Dearest, I once would have sold my soul for the price of a passionate kiss ;

Dearest, you know what your lover was when the songs
 of his youth were sung ;
Dearest, the devil deserves your soul for driving me
 down to this.

YOU AND I.

SPARE your censures, worthy friend, on my love of
    drinking ;
Shut your senses, if you please, to the glasses clinking.

Only, while you rest with me, prithee keep your curses
For some other fellow's wine, other fellow's verses.

By what frenzy of reproof is your wisdom bitten ?
Are the sins that I commit in your volume written ?

If I run a tavern score, you don't pay the reckoning ;
If the Lotus-maiden nods, not to you she's beckoning.

Who shall say behind the Veil which is good and evil ?
Who shall say if you or I journey to the devil ?

Very varied laws of life you and I are firm on ;
Which of us, my friend, is text ? which of us is sermon ?

Every sober man or drunk seeks his soul's ideal ;
In the tavern and the mosque love alike is real.

Paradise is fair indeed ; but this side of heaven
There is joy in noonday sun, joy in shades of even.

Be not boastful of thy worth, for who knows when
    mounted
To the final judgment-seat how his sum is counted?

Sanctimonious folk like you, filled with moral phrases,
May be sent, to your surprise, packing off to blazes;

While poor rogues like us, who drink ere the vintage
    fail us,
May be plucked to Paradise from this very alehouse.

CONSOLATION.

Weep not for the lost Yusuf, in Canaan his eyes shall close;
Weep not for your wasted garden, it shall blossom like the rose.

Weep not for your nights of revel, weep not for your days of tears,
For an hour's repentance cancels all the sins of sixty years.

Weep not, soul with sorrow laden, once again the spring returns ;
Singer of the night, your planet once again in heaven burns.

Weep not for your boyhood's passions, weep not for your youth's despair ;
Every poet's heart was tangled sometime in a woman's hair.

Weep not, watcher for to-morrow, that thou never canst prevail
With the stars to tell the secret shrouded up behind the Veil.

Weep not if life's gloomy pathway terrifies your wandering soul,
For the byeway, not the highway, best conducteth to the goal.

Weep not for the loss of brother, grieve not at the gain of foe ;
Would you with Allah be angry when the winds of winter blow ?

Weep not, Hafiz, poor and lonely, but not all unhappy man,
While your life's as true and upright as ordained by Alkoran.

LOTUS.

I LOVE the Lotus-blossom when it wreathes
   Its painted petals in my sweetheart's tresses,
And she, enchanted by its odour, breathes
   Soft words of love, and soothes with soft caresses.

I love the Lotus-blossom when it lies
   On the white bosom of a sleeping woman,
And falls and rises as the dreamer sighs,
   For that love's sake she yet has told to no man.

I love the Lotus-blossom, for it grows
    On a lone grave beside a silent river ;
There my youth's mistress takes her last repose :
    I loved, I hated, and I now forgive her.

PHILOSOPHY FOR OTHERS.

SALUTE the summer, breathe the breath of God,
   Be happy while you can, for by-and-by
   You that are now so full of life must die,
And redder roses blossom from your sod.

Believe me, brother, that behind the Veil
   A harp is touched, and one is singing to it
   A song of counsel, if you only knew it;
When wilt thou list, and let that song prevail?

Ask not poor Hafiz to admonish you
    With whom you should frequent, with whom be drinking,
    For surely half an hour of tranquil thinking
Will teach you better what you ought to do.

The road that leads us to the Friend at last
    Is hard to travel, full of fear, temptation;
    But think, my brother, think of the elation
In looking back along the road you've past.

Cease this perplexing problem to revolve;
    Him the world clutches with a thousand fingers
    Who on the pathway of his purpose lingers
To solve the riddle none were meant to solve.

For every flower that in the meadow blows,
   Is like a book God opened to confess on
   His secret purpose. But canst read the lesson
Writ in the purple petals of the rose?

And yet, O Hafiz! thou that talkest so wise
   Of prudence, and of patience, and compassion,
   Thy heart is all on fire with foolish passion
For one fair face and two tormenting eyes.

WISDOM.

Weep not for the waning rose
Sigh not when the south wind blows,
Drown reflection in the can,
Dissipated Mussulman;
Better to be glad than sad,
By the waves of Rocknabad.

If the truth must be confest,
Youth's a juggle, love's a jest,

Life's a comic caravan,
Discontented Mussulman;
Better to be glad than sad,
By the waves of Rocknabad.

Eat your crust and drink your wine,
Deem the girl you love divine,
Make you merry for a span,
Philosophic Mussulman;
Better to be glad than sad,
By the waves of Rocknabad.

RENUNCIATION.

Thus Allah makes proclamation:
   Ye that seek for peace of mind,
   What ye seek will only find
In the word renunciation.

Must I spill the wine I'm drinking,
   Must I practise what I preach,
   Ere Mohammed's hand will reach
Out to save my soul from sinking?

Must I shrink from soft caresses,
  Must I turn my eyes away,
  Must my heart no longer stay
In the tangle of your tresses?

Talk no more; I'll not believe it;
  Love is far too sweet to lose,
  And while wine is in the cruse,
By my beard I'll never leave it.

Hafiz, if the dedication
  Of thy being must belong
  Thus to woman, wine, and song,
Cease to preach renunciation.

AFTER RHAMAZAN.

THANK Allah! the fast is over;
   Thank Allah! the feast is here;
And at last each jolly lover
Of the vintage lives in clover
   Through the sweetest of the year.

Hide thy visage, sour ascetic;
   Go thy ways, thy hour has past;
While all revellers poetic
Join in union sympathetic,
   Drinking full and drinking fast.

After Rhamazan

Why should I incur reproaches
   If I like a stoup of wine?
Thank Allah! the hour approaches
When the jolly tapster broaches
   Liquor more than half divine.

He that drains a decent flagon
   At the wine house, can ignore
How the tongues of envy wag on.
Think how dull their days must drag on,
   Who run up no wine-house score.

For Allah's illumination,
   Shining on this rosy tide,

Finds no smug dissimulation,
  Calling out for reprobation,
    Fair without and foul inside.

Clean our lives, our language civil,
  Alkoran's law understood;
And we never let the devil
Catch us calling good things evil,
  And the things of evil good.

Where's the harm of my carouses
  With the vineyard's sanguine flood?
If I drink till dawn arouses
All the Muftis from their houses,
  Do I drink my brother's blood?

After Rhamazan

Hafiz, cease thy soul to trouble
    With the wherefore and the how ;
Laugh and love, for life's a bubble ;
Drink till everything grows double,
    And the roses leave your brow.

LONELY.

I AM lonely, very lonely, for the girl who stole my heart
Shines a star in other heavens, plays another lover's part,
While I sit in sombre silence, hearing how my heart will beat,
When I catch the faintest footfall sounding down my dreary street.
Is it she, or else some message sent from her to soothe my pain,
Falling on the thirsty seeds of passion like a holy rain?

No, the sounds die out in silence, and the twilight deepens down,
And the orisons of evening breathe above the darkening town;
But my mosque is not the Mufti's, for my beacon in the gloom
Is the crimson lamp-light floating from the tavern's warmest room.
There I sit and drug my sorrow to a sleep that seems like death,
There forget that I have ever kissed her lips and felt her breath
From the parted smiling petals of the rose-flower of her mouth
Breathe upon my eyes and hair the perfumes of the odorous south.

It is war 'twixt wine and memory; on the tavern's trampled sill
I will plant my colours proudly, ruddy as the drops that fill
Yonder jars, whose prisoned magic slays regret and saps desire,
Burning folly from my bosom with the vineyard's liquid fire.
Woe is me! I boast untimely; even as I lift the cup,
On the purple flood the face of the beloved comes floating up.

COURAGE.

My soul rose out of its sleep, and said
There were angels once, but they all are dead ;
And heaven is empty, and cold and grey
As a world whose heat has burnt away.

The leaves of the tree of life are shed,
The bird who sang in the boughs has fled,
The coffin of night shrouds the corpse of the day,
And winter withers the mirth of May.

Allah and Shitan have gone to bed,
The prophets and saints are lapped in lead,
The shrines are shattered and no men pray,
The law is broken and none obey.

The roses of youth are no longer red,
Bitter life's wine is, bitter its bread,
The lips of the poets are stopped with clay,
And beauty fades into dull decay.

Then I turned me to Alkoran and read,
And Mohammed whispered, ' Hold up thy head.
Sin is an enemy hard to slay ;
Cry Allah 'l 'Akbar, and fight your way.'

VINE-VISIONS.

WHILE the House of Hope is builded on the weak and shifting sand,
While our breath is as the wind is, take the flagon in your hand;

For while I was quaffing, laughing in the tavern yester-night,
From the unknown world an angel floated on my swimming sight—

Handed me a golden vessel, bade me drink, and as I
   drank
All my swooning senses straightway in the pool of
   slumber sank;

And I dreamed a dream enchanted of a land beyond
   the sky,
Where no youthful cheek grows paler, where no flagon
   e'er runs dry,

Where no woman whispers falsely, where no eyes are
   ever wet,
Where no kisses ever weary, where no loving hearts
   forget.

Then I woke, and wept at waking, leaving in that pleasant land
Fairer flowers than Mosellay has, bluer domes than Samarcand.

Nevermore, unhappy Hafiz, will you tread that pleasant land,
Though you sucked the Seven Oceans from their cup of golden sand.

A DREAM.

I DREAMT, about the morning hours,
That in a field of scented flowers,
  By Rocknabad's cool flow,
  I saw Ferangis go
Swift by me like a dream of spring;
And I, whose heart was hot to fling
  Myself before my dear,
  Stood full of silent fear.

A Dream

And then I dreamt she came to lay
Softly her hand in mine and say,
  ' Hafiz, you yet shall know
  How happy is your woe;
For what gift can the silent years
Offer so precious as these tears,
  And memory of the ache
  Your heart had for my sake?'

Then, seeming stirred by pitying thought
Of all the joy I vainly sought,
  You gave your hand to kiss,
  Saying, ' Remember this

When you and I are grey and old,
When all this fiery love is cold,
  And, honouring lost delight,
   Keep your soul's whiteness white.'

I had no power to speak or move;
Slowly the image of my love
  Faded before my eyes
   Like light from summer skies.
I wake and find Ferangis gone,
Yet scarce believe I am alone;
  One minute since my hand
   Had touched her where I stand.

A Dream

I read of men whom love made mad
In antique legends, softly sad
  As wind is after rain.
  I weep for Saadi's pain,
And stir the dust that lies above
Long shelves of poets crossed in love,
  To gain from their disgrace
  Some comfort for my case.

I find fit voices for my grief
In many a buried poet's leaf;
  But, ah! what ancient song
  Contains a charm so strong

That it shall make your heart confess
You love me, neither more or less?
    Which learning, surely I
    Might be content to die.

And yet, when I reflect how fair
Those almond eyes and sable hair
    And gracious body are,
    I cry, ' Out of my star
Such beauty is ; ' I am as one
Who dreams of kingdoms till the sun
    Warns, if he would be fed,
    To rise and beg his bread.

A Dream

Soft voices whisper in my ears,
'What girl deserves the grace of tears?
  Courage! the world is wide;
  Life's best is to be tried.
If this love fail, fresh loves await;
The reddest roses blossom late.
  Have you not passed before
  Out of love's curtained door?'

ATTAR OF LOVE.

THERE is neither pledge nor pity in the beauty of the rose
For the nightingale, whose sorrow in melodious madness flows ;

Though the brown bird sang for ever till its singing spirit fled,
Still the rose would greet the west wind with its petals' perfect red.

Once a songster in the garden chanted to a scornful rose,
'Cease thy scorn, for in the hedges many a fairer blossom grows.'

Then the rose made answer smiling, 'Singer, thou hast spoken sooth,
But no lover e'er addresses lover with so little ruth.

'Think not how the roses wither, be but gay while roses bloom,
For the world's delight is little in the shadow of the tomb.'

Hafiz, if you sang more sweetly than the wind among the reeds,
She you love is but the rose tree, and the rose tree never heeds.

VAULTING AMBITION.

ONCE in my way an Arab story came
   Relating how a poet, drugged with wine,
   Watched from the tavern door where the divine
Pale moon lit all the sky with silver flame;
And crying, 'By Allah's eternal name,
   I swear that argent splendour shall be mine!'
   Leaped, clutching at the sky, and rolled supine
A muddy rascal, steeped in mire and shame.

This is our common madness. Am not I
    Moon-haunted by thy beauty? Yet I stand
No farther from the empress of the sky
    Than from one touch of thy all-conquering hand ;
And though my songs made all the heavens sigh,
    I know you will not pity, nor understand.

A NIGHT-PIECE.

ONCE at night I paced my garden, seeking—but I sought in vain—
From the perfume of the roses balsam for my burning brain;

For through all that dusk the circle of a single damask bloom
Shone more brightly than the cresset on a true believer's tomb;

And so haughty in the splendour of her beauty burned this rose,
That she banished from the bosom of the nightingale repose,

While the eyes of sad narcissus floated o'er with loving tears,
And the tulip bared her bosom wounded by a thousand spears.

Vainly then the lily offered to console the poet's care,
Vainly too the violet pleaded, 'Are no other blossoms fair?'

Since the only potent rival of the rose tree is the vine,
Let me drown my hopeless passion in the Seven Seas of wine.

' Hafiz, I conjure thee, from the rose tree pluck thy heart away.'
Lo, the message is delivered, and the bearer speeds away.

FALLEN ANGELS.

'TIS written in the Writing how a pair
Of angels dwelt with children of the dust,
And judged between the just and the unjust;
   Loyal to God, until a woman, fair
   As sun or stars, entangled in her hair
The hearts of those twin angels, and dark lust
Consumed them, till they whispered, 'Surely must
   We temper justice to a thing so rare.'
God punished those false angels, yet if I
   Were placed like them upon some judgment-seat

Speaking the law, and you came wandering by,
  One smile of yours would fling me at your feet
  Crying, ' Have pity upon me, O most sweet !
Do with me as you will, and let me die.'

PRAISE OF WINE.

ONCE again the ruddy vintage storms the chambers of
  my brain,
Steals my senses with its kisses, steals and yet shall steal
  again ;

But I do not blame the grape's blood for the vengeances
  it wreaks
When it plants its purple standard on the stronghold of
  my cheeks.

May Allah confer his blessing on the hands that pluck
   the grape,
May their footsteps never fail who tread its clusters out
   of shape.

Since the love of wine was written by Fate's finger on
   my brow,
What is written once is written, and you cannot change
   it now;

Talk no babble about wisdom: in the awful hour of
   death,
Is the breath of Aristotle better than the beggar's
   breath?

Spare me, pious friend, reproaches, for the selfsame God who chose
You to be so wise and pious, made me love the wine and rose.

Hafiz, spend thy life so wisely that when thou at last art dead,
'Dead' may not be all the comment, all the requiem that's said.

HAROUN ER-RASHEED'S POET.

KHALIFAH HAROUN, surnamed Er-Rasheed,
   In the calm evening of a festal day,
   Ordered his bard, Abu-l'Atahiyeh,
To praise the life it pleased his lord to lead.

The poet bowed and stirred the silver wires,
   And sang, 'Khalifah, peace and pleasure wait
   Within the shadow of your palace gate,
And deep fulfilment of your heart's desires.'

Said Haroun, smiling, 'Here is silver speech
   That shall be sealed with silver; speak again,
   And find my bounty boundless as the main
Which knows, so poets say, no further beach.'

Again the poet's voice and lute allied,
   'Let not the day star nor the night star shine
   Upon the hour that leaves a wish of thine,
Thy lightest wish, Haroun, ungratified.'

Still Haroun smiled, 'This time thy words are gold,
   And shall be guerdoned with a golden fee;
   Sing on, sweet voice, sing on and comfort me,
Nor ever fear to find thy master cold.'

Then sang Abu-l'Atahiyeh aloud,
   'In those dark moments when thy faltering breath
   Shall strive in vain against all-conquering death,
These things shall seem like shadows on a shroud.'

There fell a fearful silence on the place,
   While the scared guests saw Haroun from his throne
   Frown at the bard, and then, with a deep groan,
Hide in his trembling hands his weeping face.

Straightway a supple courtier standing by
   Cried to the singer, 'Blasted be the throat
   Which frights our master with a boding note
In lieu of mirthful music; look to die.'

'Nay,' Haroun whispered, 'do not blame the bard;
  He saw our soul benighted, and, like wind,
  Dispersed the veil of error. Let him find
My richest gems too poor for his reward.'

GHAZEL.

If the gracious girl I worship would but take my heart in hand,
I would give her for her beauty Ispahan and Samarcand.

But this lass, the very fairest trouble of our tranquil town,
Plucks all patience from my bosom, lifts my hopes to laugh them down.

She has slandered me, so be it; I forgive her, speaking sooth,
For the harshest words fall softly from the scarlet lips of youth;

Yet I dare not call her cruel, though she does me grievous wrong,
For what lovely face is flattered by the proudest poet's song?

Fill, then, friend, while wine remaineth, for in Paradise, dear lad,
We shall sigh for Mosellay and weep the waves of Rocknabad.

Speak of wine and song and women; cease, I pray, to seek in vain,
What that mystery most mystic called to-morrow may contain.

String thy pearls and sing them, Hafiz, for from heaven's golden bars
God has shed upon thy verses all the sweetness of the stars.

THE GRAVE OF OMAR-I-KHAYYAM.

I, NAMED Nizami, child of Samarcand,
The holy place whose towers aspire to heaven,
Whose domes are blue as heaven's inverted cup,
The consecrated shrine, head of Islam,
Whose heart is at Meccah, the happy spot
Where bloom the gardens of the Heart's Delight,
Where in the house upon the Shepherd's Hill
Wise men pursue the pathway of the stars —
I, even Nizami, write this record down
In God's name, merciful, compassionate,
A proof of his compassion.

               When my youth
Burned in my body like a new-fed flame,
When wisdom seemed an easy flower to pluck,
And knowledge fruit that ripens in a day;
Ah me! that merry When so long ago
I was a pupil of that man of men,
Omar, the tent-maker of Naishapur,
That is Khorassan's crown, Omar the wise,
Whose wisdom read the golden laws of life,
And made them ours for ever in his songs,
Omar the star-gazer.
                     One day by chance,
I taxing all my student's store of wit
With thought of is and is not, good and bad,
And fondly dreaming that my fingers soon

Would close upon the key of heaven and earth,
I met my master in a garden walk,
Musing as was his wont, I knew not what,
Perhaps some better mode of marshalling
Those daily soldiers of the conquering years,
Perchance some subtler science which the stars
Ciphered in fire upon the vaulted sky
For him alone, perchance on some rare rhymes
Pregnant with mighty thoughts, or on some girl,
Star-eyed and cypress-slender, tulip-cheeked
And jasmine-bosomed, for he loved such well,
And deemed it wisdom.
     Omar saw me not,
And would have passed me curtained in his
 thoughts ;

But I, perked up with youthful consequence
At mine own wisdom, plucked him by the sleeve,
And with grave salutation, as befits
The pupil to the master, stayed his course
And craved his patience.
      Omar gazed at me
With the grave sweetness which his servants loved,
And gave me leave to speak, which I, on fire
To tell the thing I thought, made haste to do,
And poured my babble in the master's ear
Of solving human doubt.
      When I had done,
And, panting, looked into my master's eyes
To read therein approval of my plan,
He turned his head, and for a little while

THE GRAVE OF OMAR-I-KHAYYAM

Waited in silence, while my petulant mind
Galloped again the course of argument
And found no flaw, all perfect.
      Still he stood
Silent, and I, the riddle-reader, vexed
At long-delayed approval, touched again
His sleeve, and with impatient reverence
Said,
  ' Master, speak, that I may garner up
In scented manuscripts the thoughts of price
That fall from Omar's lips.'
      He smiled again
In sweet forgiveness of my turbulent mood,
And with a kindly laughter in his eyes
He said,

'I have been thinking, when I die,
That I should like to slumber where the wind
May heap my tomb with roses.'
                                      So he spoke,
And then with thoughtful face and quiet tread
He past and left me staring, most amazed
At such a pearl from such a sea of thought,
And marvelling that great philosophers
Can pay so little sometimes heed to truth
When truth is thrust before them. God be praised!
I am wiser now, and grasp no golden key.

Years came and went, and Omar passed away,
First from those garden walks of Samarcand
Where he and I so often watched the moon

Silver the bosoms of the cypresses,
And so from out the circle of my life,
And in due season out of life itself;
And his great name became a memory
That clung about me like the scent of flowers
Beloved in boyhood, and the wheeling years
Ground pleasure into dust beneath my feet;
And so the world wagged till there came a day
When I that had been young and was not young,
I found myself in Naishapur, and there
Bethought me of my master dead and gone,
And the musk-scented preface of my youth.
Then to myself I said, 'Nizami, rise
And seek the tomb of Omar.'
                      So I sought,

And after seeking found, and, lo! it lay
Beyond a garden full of roses, full
As the third heaven is full of happy eyes;
And every wind that whispered through the trees
Scattered a heap of roses on his grave;
Yea, roses leaned, and from their odorous hearts
Rained petals on his marble monument,
Crimson as lips of angels.
                              'Then my mind,
Sweeping the desert of departed years,
Leaped to that garden speech in Samarcand,
The cypress grove, my fretful questioning,
And the mild beauty of my master's face.
Then I knelt down and glorified Allah,
Who is compassionate and merciful,

That of his boundless mercy he forgave
This singing sinner; for I surely knew
That all the leaves of every rose that dripped
Its tribute on the tomb where Omar sleeps,
Were tears and kisses that should smooth away
His record of offence; for Omar sinned,
Since Omar was a man.
      He wished to sleep
Beneath a veil of roses; Heaven heard,
Forgave, and granted, and the perfumed pall
Hides the shrine's whiteness. Glory to Allah!

OMAR ANSWERS.

Now by the memory of Kai Khosru,
Of Kaikobad, of Zal and Rustem too,
   O English singer rousing me from sleep,
The student of the stars will answer you.

For what avails it cycles to have lain
Since first the roses gushed their scented rain
   Upon my grave in Naishapur if men
In the world's winter take my name in vain?

Through piled-up earth and ages echoes reach
My tranquil slumbers of an alien speech,
Blown over seas wherein strange doctors preach
Strange sermons on the things I thought to teach.

For, misinterpreting the songs I sung,
By vain desire and vain ambition stung,
  O for one hour of that lost age ! they cry,
That golden age when old Khayyam was young.

Fools who believe the world was otherwise
Than what it now is in the Persian's eyes,
  Or think the secret of content was found
Beneath the canopy of Persian skies.

Man is to-day what man was yesterday—
Will be to-morrow; let him curse or pray,
   Drink or be dull, he learns not nor shall learn
The lesson that will laugh the world away.

The world as grey or just as golden shows,
The wine as sweet or just as bitter flows,
   For you as me; and you, like me, may find
Perfume or canker in the reddest rose.

The tale of life is hard to understand;
But while the cup waits ready to your hand,
   Drink and declare the summer roses blow
As red in London as in Samarcand.

Lips are as sweet to kiss and eyes as bright
As ever fluttered Omar with delight ;
   English or Persian, while the mouth is fair,
What can it matter how it says good-night ?

Whether the legend in the Book of Youth
Runs left or right, it reads a prayer for ruth ;
   The music of the bird upon the bough
Meant, and still means, no more nor less than truth.

The wisdom of the wisest of the wise
Is but the pinch of powder in the eyes
   Thrown by the fingers of the fiend, that we
True things from false may fail to recognise.

And not a pang which vexes human flesh,
And not a problem which the Sufis thresh,
   But scared my body or perplexed my soul,
And what I felt each man must feel afresh.

So, brother, by Allah! forbear to weep:
Life is a wine which you may drink as deep
   As ever I did, for the hour will come
When you, like old Khayyam, will fall asleep.

Therefore, O northern singer! prithee cease
To vex my sprite with questions. Know, thy lease
   Was by the selfsame Master made as mine;
Be patient, then, and let me sleep in peace.

تم الكتاب

[To-day a rose tree grown of a seedling brought from the grave of Omar Khayyám at Naishapur, and grafted on an English stem, will be planted on the grave of Edward Fitzgerald, Omar's translator, at Boulge.]

From Naishapur to England, from the tomb
Where Omar slumbers to the Narrow Room
That shrines Fitzgerald's ashes, Persia sends
Perfume and Pigment of her Rose to bloom.

Wedded with Rose of England, for a sign
That English lips, transmuting the divine
High-piping music of the song that ends,
As it began, with Wine and Wine and Wine.

Across the ages caught the words that fell
From Omar's mouth and made them audible
To the unnumbered sitters at Life's Feast
Who wear their hearts out over Heaven and Hell.

Vex not to-day with wonder which were best,
The Student, Scholar, Singer of the West,
Or Singer, Scholar, Student of the East—
The soul of Omar burned in England's breast.

And howsoever Autumn's breezes blow
About this Rose, and Winter's fingers throw,
In mockery of Oriental noons,
Upon this grass the monumental snow;

Still in our dreams the Eastern Rose survives
Lending diviner fragrance to our lives:
The World is old, cold, warned by waning moons,
But Omar's creed in English verse revives.

The fountain in the tulip-tinted dale,
The manuscript of some melodious tale
Babbling of love and lover's passion-pale,
Of Rose, of Cypress, and of Nightingale;

The cup that Saki proffers to our lips,
The cup from which the Rose-Red Mercy drips,
Bidding forget how, like a sinking sail,
Day after day into the darkness slips;

The wisdom that the Watcher of the Skies
Won from the wandering stars that soothed his eyes,
The legend writ below, around, above—
"One thing at least is certain, this Life flies;"

These were the gifts of Omar—these he gave
Full-handed; his Disciple sought to save
Some portion for his people, and their love
Plants Omar's Rose upon an English grave.

J. H. McC.

www.ingramcontent.com/pod-product-compliance
Lightning Source LLC
Chambersburg PA
CBHW031118160426
43192CB00008B/1036